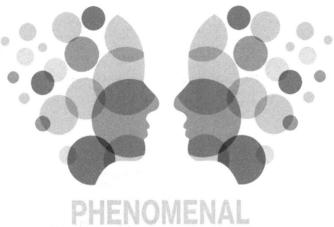

PHENOMENAL
YOU+H

The 7 Lies Between You and Success

ISBN: 978-1-946629-97-5

To Jessica Hunter

To Jessica, although you are no longer here on this earth with us, I hope somehow you can hear this message. If not now, when you and I are reunited in heaven.

I have to begin by telling you "I'm sorry." The last time I saw you, you were with us at The Destin Dream Retreat with your parents. I was busy, and I didn't slow down long enough to have the "phenomenal talk" with you personally. I didn't pause long enough to get to know you.

I regret that.

When a tragedy like yours strikes a community, one thinks, "Is there something I could have done?" For me, I think, "Maybe if I had spent time with Jessica, she would not have listened to the wrong voice on that fateful night."

I'm sure everyone that knew you has similar thoughts. I know that you and your parents would say something that would make me feel better, but I will always regret not spending more time talking to you.

But because of you, my passion to help kids has become stronger, and more urgent. My goal now is to slow down for every young one to have the phenomenal talk with them. Because of you, there is a work called I Know Jessica. Because of you, many young people will be saved from listening to the wrong voices, and many will be helped by listening to the right voices.

When I see you in heaven, we'll have that phenomenal talk together.
Your friend in Christ,

Howard Partridge

FOREWORD
By Alan Hunter
(Jessica's Dad)

It was still pitch dark outside as the pounding on the door awoke Debbie and me in the early morning hours of October 6, 2014. As we peeked out the door before opening it, I could see that there were two police officers standing there. My heart started pounding and it was difficult to breathe. In just a few seconds, we heard words no parent ever wants to hear. "Are you the parents of Jessica Hunter?"

All they could tell us was that Jessica was in critical condition and they gave us the number of the hospital. My mind wondered if she had been in an accident on her way back to San Marcos, TX, after visiting friends in Austin. We were not prepared for what came next.

After a brief discussion with the ER nurse, Debbie and I quickly threw on clothes and started our three-hour drive to Austin to be by Jessica's side. We found out that she had a bad reaction to taking a drug while she attended the Austin City Music Festival the previous evening.

The next two days were a blur. After initially hearing that Jessica's brain activity was good, her vital signs and organ functions grew worse. She never recovered and in the early morning hours of October 8, 2014, Jessica, our only child, died.

On the long drive home, Debbie and I discussed what no parent wants to ever talk about, their child's funeral service. We also wondered how this happened to Jessica. She was not a drug user. She was a happy, active, caring person. We discovered that curiosity got the best of her, and she made a terrible decision to try the drug commonly referred to as Molly with some friends.

It was then that we decided that something had to be done. Jessica's life was too important to let her story end this way. We knew that she wouldn't want others to make the same bad decision and she'd be the first person to tell others not to do what she had done.

During this time, I was fortunate to be involved in Howard Partridge's organization, Phenomenal Products, Inc., to grow my home services business. It is truly a community founded on Godly principles and everyone there has a passionate desire to help others succeed.

During our time at the hospital with Jessica, a member of Howard's Inner Circle community brought us a food care package. In addition, in the days following Jessica's death, I received dozens of phone calls, text messages, and cards from other community members all expressing their condolences and offers to help in any way they could.

A few days after Jessica's memorial service, Howard called me to see how he and his community could help. As we talked and cried together, we talked about what the future would hold. Howard encouraged me to think about how this affected the dreams I had for the future. He promised to be there to help in any way he could… and he and his Inner Circle Community have been there to encourage and support us along the way.

It was at one of Howard's quarterly events that I met Tom Ziglar, CEO, Ziglar Inc., which helps individuals and companies to achieve higher levels of success and significance.

As Debbie and I developed the I Know Jessica Drug-Awareness project, it became clear to me when I talked with high school and college young people that they are receiving mixed messages from society and what was needed was the right type of organizations and communities to help them navigate their way into adulthood.

As a result, I have read everything written by Howard and Tom. I have attended their events, talked with them, prayed with them, become friends with them. These relationships have encouraged us to further spread the I Know Jessica message which led to the establishment of The Jessica Hunter Foundation, Inc., a 501(c)(3) non-profit organization in 2019 that teaches young people, their parents, educators, and other concerned adults about the dangers of drugs and provides solutions to help young adults in understanding themselves, having better relationships with others, and establishing and reaching their goals in life.

In today's world there is so much noise. It can be confusing for adults and is utterly perplexing for younger people. It's critical to filter out the noise and focus on the truth. It's been said, "It takes a village to raise a child," but the truth is that it takes the "Right Village."

I am excited about this book and how it will help you in raising your child or influencing the young people in your lives. You will discover in the pages that follow that it is part of the "Right Village."

Alan Hunter
Jessica's Dad
Founder of The Jessica Hunter Foundation Inc.
Certified Human Behavior Consultant in association with Personality Insights, Inc.
Certified Ziglar Legacy Coach

Lifetime Member of Howard Partridge's Inner Circle
www.IKnowJessica.com
www.IKnowJessica.org

Contents

Introduction: You've Been LIED To **11**

Chapter 1: You Aren't Good Enough to Be Successful **19**

Chapter 2: You Aren't Smart Enough to Be Successful **35**

Chapter 3: You Aren't Attractive Enough to Be Successful **49**

Chapter 4: You Aren't Connected Enough to Be Successful **55**

Chapter 5: You Aren't Important Enough to Be Successful **67**

Chapter 6: You Aren't Rich Enough to Be Successful **77**

Chapter 7: You Aren't Free Enough to Be Successful **95**

Acknowledgments: 103

INTRODUCTION
You've Been LIED To

Have you ever been lied to?

Have you ever had someone lie *about* you?

How does that make you feel? Does it make you mad? Does it hurt? Do you feel let down? And what if the person who lied is someone you really trusted?

What if I told you that you're being lied to every day? What if you're being lied to about things that really matter to you? What if I told you there are seven specific lies that you've most likely believed? And what if those lies are keeping you from having the success you were created to have?

Before I share the lies, let me share why I'm writing to you, and why this message is so important for you to hear.

There are three reasons I'm writing to you…

First, I'm sharing this message with you because God told me to. "Oh, God talks to you, Howard?" Yes, in fact, once God spoke to me AUDIBLY. What's more important is that He wants to talk to you too!

More on that later, but seriously, why should you listen to a 60-year-old-ancient-man-with-old-fashioned-values like me? What could we possibly have in common?

Even though there isn't a better reason than "God told me to," the second reason I am writing to you is because I was once where you are right now. I know how you feel. When I was your age, I believed the lies you are probably living right now. Because of the lies, I became a bad kid. When I became a teenager, my life got WORSE! Why? More lies!

I have also had a unique view on the damage the lies are doing to our world. Born in 1960, television was just becoming popular, and that was followed by a great rebellion that has ruined many things for you. Since you are a younger person, you can't see it because you didn't have a front row seat like I did.

So, sit back and let Mr. Phenomenal tell you what happened. I'll tell you about the lies, and I'll tell you some crazy stories too!

You may not be a bad kid like I was, but the lies you have believed are probably hurting you right now or will hurt you in the future. I care about this world, and you are our future.

So I want to tell you the truth so you can not only be more successful, but our world can be a better place to live.

Finally, the reason I'm writing to you is because I have what you want!

Okay, "Mr. Phenomenal," first you said you were where I am at my age. Now you're telling me that you have what I want? You don't even know me. How could you possibly know what I want and how I feel? How can you say those things if you don't even know me?

Test me and see...

Over the past six decades, I've learned that everyone wants the same nine things out of life. I learned these nine things from a man more ancient than me. A man with a very funny name.

His name was Zig Ziglar. He was 86 when he passed away, but he was a LIVING LEGEND! In fact, he is still a legend today. He is the most quoted motivational speaker on earth. If you ask your parents, teachers, or coaches who he is, they have probably heard of him.

He grew up very poor in Mississippi, but he became one of the highest paid and in-demand public speakers in the world. He got paid a *hundred thousand dollars* just for *one* speech! He is known around the world and is the most quoted motivational speaker on planet earth.

I learned from Mr. Ziglar that we all want the same nine things out of life. So, put me to the test.

Just verbally say to yourself "YES" or "NO" after each of these nine things:

1. To be happy Y/N
2. To be healthy Y/N
3. To be prosperous (to have money) Y/N
4. To have friends Y/N
5. To have peace of mind Y/N
6. To have good family relationships Y/N
7. To be secure Y/N
8. To have hope for the future Y/N
9. To be loved, valued, and appreciated Y/N

In just a bit, I'll share how to get *exactly* what you want personally, but let's stay with what everyone wants for now. After all, everyone includes you! Would you agree that most people (young or old) don't have all nine of those things in life?

Instead, this is what it looks like for many people…

1. Unhappy, unfulfilled, bored.
2. Unhealthy. Overweight, maybe even obese.
3. Little to no money of their own. In debt. Barely able to make their monthly bills. Or so much money that it has caused other major problems in their life.
4. Few real friends (regardless of social media numbers or fame).
5. Constant stress, anxiety, and fear.
6. Strained relationships - don't feel understood or valued.
7. Insecure and maybe even depressed.
8. Little hope that things will change for the better.
9. Don't feel loved, accepted, or important.

Look around. Would you agree that many people's lives resemble the second list? What about you? Have you suffered from any of the things in the second list? Take a moment to think about it.

So, Howard, are you telling me that you have ALL nine of the things that everyone wants out of life?

YEP!

I have lots of true friends, and I have *lots* of fun, and I have a phenomenal relationship with God. I mean seriously, I already told you that God *spoke* to me audibly! And He loves me!

What if I told you that I have more money than I need, I can go anywhere in the world I want, anytime I want, that I have phenomenal houses, phenomenal cars, *and* I have a loving family?

I have all nine of the things everyone wants in life.

But it didn't start out that way…

I'm originally from L.A. (Lower Alabama!) There were seven kids crammed into a little six-hundred-square-foot- shack with a roof that leaked so bad we had to get out all the pots and pans to catch the leaks when it rained.

There was only *one* teeny-tiny bathroom that didn't even have a bathtub. It had a small shower. The shack was on concrete blocks, and the shower was made from a little pad of concrete with tile on it. One day, my stepdad stepped into the shower and the entire floor fell through to the ground under the house.

We didn't have money to fix it, so we propped up the broken shower floor on a big tree stump under the house as a platform. This left a four-inch crack between the floor and the rotted-out sheetrock. If you dropped the soap and it bounced the wrong way, it ended up under the house, *in the dirt!*

At one point, my mother fed us on a hundred dollars a month

from the welfare department. I don't care when that was, it just wasn't a lot of money. My real father left when I was only a year old, and I had two stepfathers after that.

When you grow up in an environment like that, what are you likely to turn out like? At almost 18 years old, I was a rebellious teenager and got kicked out of the house by my second stepdad. I deserved it, I guess. I was a wild kid, and looking back on the situation, I have to give him credit for taking on seven kids and getting us off welfare.

I had *no* money when I got kicked out. I stayed at my best friend's house that night and scraped up enough money for a Greyhound bus ticket to Houston, TX, the next night. Why Houston? My real dad, who left when I was only a year old, had recently been to visit, and he even bought me a suitcase. My sister was there, and I heard that Houston was booming. I figured I could get a fresh start there.

The next morning, I stepped off the bus with only twenty-five cents in my pocket. I wasn't sure if my dad would be there to pick me up. After all, I had not asked him for permission to come. I just told him I was coming. What I *was* sure about was that my sister would find a way. I just knew I had to get out of the situation I was in.

So, how did I get from there to where I am today?

I'm gonna tell you! And I'm gonna tell you those seven lies that you've been told that are keeping you from having the nine things you really want out of life.

And I'll share the seven truths that will set you free! I'll help you find your purpose, your passion, and your path in a confusing, chaotic world.

Are you ready?

Let's go!

CHAPTER 1
You Aren't Good Enough to Be Successful

On September 15, 1960, Hurricane Ethel was brewing up her wrath in the Gulf of Mexico, bearing down on the southern town of Mobile, Alabama. I was born during that storm. Hurricane Ethel didn't do much damage, but Hurricane Howard sure did!

But there was a more dangerous and destructive storm brewing in America. This was a storm like no other in the history of the world. For the first time ever, live television streamed into the living rooms of America. And what started out as a good thing ended up being the biggest tool ever to spread lies faster than ever before.

Then came the internet and social media. With social media, anyone can put their voice out into the world. Whether it's a foreign government that wants to control our thoughts, our own government, big tech themselves, celebrities or companies, or some guy in his basement, it's hard to know who to believe.

Strangers on a screen (who we think we know) who seem like they have our best interest at heart have worked hard to addict us and tell us the truth *they* want us to believe. Recently, the top people from social media companies admitted that they have rigged social media to addict us. So-called friends spread lies that really hurt other people, even causing young people to kill themselves or kill others.

What's the point? The point is the things you probably already believe are lies. For example, when our nation turned against God, the liars began to teach evolution. Now the whole world seems to believe it.

This lie was created not too long ago. Yet, it seems that most people accept that we evolved from a monkey (or a fish), that there is really no way there could be one God. And if there is a God, why is there so much suffering in the world?

In today's world, you would be considered an uneducated moron if you didn't believe in evolution, but God's Word says otherwise. And God's Word says that you were created by God and in the *image* of God. Even though a chimpanzee may have 99% of your DNA, that 1% makes all the difference in the world.

Is it possible that God somehow used evolution to create man? Is it possible that He used some of the basic building blocks that He used to create animals to create humans? Is it possible that some kind of evolutionary process was used in creation? Since I'm not a Bible scholar or scientist, I can't answer that, but I do know this...

The difference between humans and animals is that humans have a mind. A creative *mind*. Like God, you are a creator. You don't (or shouldn't) live by basic instincts alone. The mind is what separates man and beast. Your ability to *think* and *believe* makes you different than an animal.

The question is what do you believe? If you believe that you evolved from an animal and that you weren't created by God for a specific reason, then there really isn't any meaning or purpose for your life. You are a little more than an animal on this planet. Maybe the reason some people act like animals is because they believe at one time they *were* an animal!

Yes, humans have a fleshly nature, but we also have a mind that was created in the image of God. If you feel unloved, not valuable – that you don't measure up, or that you are misunderstood – that no one really knows how you feel, it can create a lot of uncertainty, stress, and anxiety about the future.

The result is a feeling of boredom. You fill your mind with endless entertainment or try to fit in by changing your identity. The reason you feel like that is that you don't know your true, phenomenal *identity.*

God made you in His Image. Man is a special creation. You have a creative mind unlike any other created being. Scripture (not religion) teaches us that you were created unique and special. God brought you and me into this world at the time that He did for a specific reason. He has a unique plan and a very special purpose for your life. God is Love, and you were made in His Image, which means you were wired for love.

Another problem is that society has convinced you that God is not real. Maybe you've seen religious people do bad things. Please keep in mind that when I talk about God, I'm not talking about religion. Religion is man-made. I'm talking about a relationship with God instead of a religion about God. That's why there are so many religions. Men wanted another way to lie and control people.

This doesn't mean that you shouldn't go to church. Jesus was the Son of God, and He sat through the "church" of His day, knowing that the people who were running it were liars. Maybe you belong to a great church.

Here's how to wade through this big mess we have created for ourselves:

Trust God. God left His Word behind for us. If you know Scripture, you know the truth. You can compare anything someone tries to tell you against the Word of God. But to be able to do that, you need to know the Scriptures.

In fact, here's what Scripture tells us...

When God made humans, He gave us our own free will, but humans have used that free will to serve ourselves rather than to love God and others. This is why you feel fear and anxiety. It all started in the Garden of Eden, when Adam and Eve were told not to eat from the tree of knowledge of good and evil. Satan showed Eve the fruit of the tree of knowledge of good and evil, and she saw that it looked good. She then reminded Satan that God said, "If you eat of this tree, you will surely die." Satan (the father of lies) questioned Eve by saying, "Did God really say that?" Does that sound familiar? It's one of culture's greatest tools – to question God.

The fall of man started with a LIE. Eve ate the fruit, and so did Adam. And two things happened. First, they did die. Not physically, but spiritually. The result is they felt fear for the first time. Before that, they had faith in God. They trusted God. He never let them down. He loved them.

Why did He give Adam and Eve their own free will? Because it would be easy for Him to create a robot. God is Love, and He wanted children who would *choose* to love Him back. So, He gave us our own will so we would love Him back.

To love God means to trust Him. To trust His Word. To trust what He said. When you know Scripture, you will know the truth. The truth will set you free. There are only two ways to live…

By God's Truth or by the ways of the world. Another way to say it is you can live by *faith* or in *fear*.

Faith comes from God. Fear comes from the world, which is controlled by demonic forces. Scripture says, "Do not be conformed to this world, but be transformed by the renewing of your mind." Our world is controlled by demonic forces that want to kill, steal, and destroy.

You may be thinking that I'm trying to preach to you right now, but here's the point:

If you want to have the nine things out of life we talked about earlier, they are not possible without God. When I lived my life separate from God, I felt no good. I wasn't truly happy. I wasn't healthy spiritually; I wasn't truly prosperous. You can have all the worldly goods, but it doesn't matter if you don't know God.

I had no true peace because the world can't offer that.

I didn't have good family relationships because I wanted to do bad things. I didn't have real friends. When I came to know Christ, all those so-called friends disappeared. I didn't feel secure because I didn't know for sure what would happen to me if I died without knowing God. I didn't have hope for the future, and I didn't know how to truly love others. I didn't feel loved like I do now.

If God created you and He created you for a reason, how will you know what that is unless you know Him? You won't.

So, let's get to the first lie:

"You aren't good enough to be successful."

This one is a little bit tricky because we are born separated from God, so we aren't naturally "good." But when you accept God into your heart, He makes you perfect. That doesn't mean you will never do anything bad again, but you will be filled with His love and His peace. The truth is that you *can* be "good" enough to be successful because He will make you new again if you trust Him. To trust Him means to follow the path that God laid out for your life, not the path of the world.

You can feel good about who God made you to be. God doesn't make any mistakes. The color of your skin or hair was not a mistake. Your appearance was not a mistake. Your gender was not a mistake. The world says it takes courage to give in to the temptations of Satan. The truth is that it takes courage to become the person God made you to be.

You were created by God. He loves you because He made you. He created you and gave you special gifts. This doesn't mean you are more important than anyone else. Everyone has been given a unique gift by God.

You have been given certain talents and abilities that no one else has. Your fingerprint is different than any of the billions of people who have come before you and the billions that may come after.

Isn't that phenomenal?

So, you are phenomenal because God made you, and everything He makes is phenomenal! He has a plan for your life. He has a specific purpose for your life. You may not know what it is for a very long time, but that's okay! You can still be successful until you find out!

You can still be happy, healthy, prosperous, have good family relationships, have a great job or career, and have great friends and lots of fun and freedom. And you can experience LOVE! The most important TRUTH any human can learn is that God is REAL, and He made you. He made you PHENOMENAL!

That brings me to the title of this book. Phenomenal You + Him = Phenomenal Success!

God created you, and He loves you. You are a child of God. Think about how much you will love your child when you have one of your own. Think about a precious newborn baby. That's how God sees you. That's how much He loves you.

God is love, and you are made in the image of God. Therefore, you are wired for love. You have the creative ability of God. You have the mind of God. You have the imagination of God. He has given you the ability to create, to love, to think, to learn, and to be the person you were created to be.

You may not believe what I'm telling you. Maybe you've done your "research." May I ask you a question? Did you research the possibility of God's existence as heavily as you did the *possibility* that He doesn't exist?

I challenge you to do that before you believe what strangers on a screen tell you. Think about why they want you to believe there is no God. If there is no God, there is no right or wrong! They can then live exactly like they want! And they can make money pushing their agenda on you.

Either one of the opposing worldviews about God takes faith. A common objection to the God theory is "Who created God?" Let me ask the God-critic a question ... "Where did the universe come from?" The answer: "It just is." My answer to the God question: He just IS. I've experienced too many miracles to deny it.

So, you can live your life believing you are a glorified animal with no control over your instincts and live without ever knowing the peace of knowing God. Never discovering the God who made you and never understanding why He made you, resulting in a meaningless life rather than a meaningful life.

Remember, I'm ancient. I know a little secret you probably don't know. Shortly after I was born, the media really took over the minds of our world. Yes, I know the government lies to us. Yes, I know that religious people act all high and mighty and do bad things. Yes, I know that many really smart people don't believe in God.

But another thing ancient Mr. Phenomenal knows is that it was the same way in Jesus' time. The religious people hated Him because He wasn't fake like them. The "intelligent" people laughed at Him because they didn't think He was very smart (like them).

What neither the religious nor intellectuals knew is that Jesus Himself actually CREATED them! How does THAT work? Well, in the beginning, God created the universe. He created the animals, and He created mankind. Jesus Christ existed from the beginning as the Son of God.

Scripture says you can do nothing good without Him, but with Him, you can become the person you were created to be. And that is what success is. It's becoming the person GOD wants you to be. When you follow that path, you will be successful, and you will have the nine things in life that everyone wants.

That's called living by faith. It's called trusting God. It's called loving God.

The world tells you that you should follow your heart. That's a mistake. Scripture says, "The heart of man is desperately wicked." You see, in the flesh, we are no good, but in Christ, we are made brand new all over again!

The world tells you to be who you want to be. God tells us to be who He made us to be.

The world says, "If it is to be, it is up to me." God says, "If it is to be, it's up to Me."

You can trust God. You cannot trust the world. Scripture says, "Let God be true and every man a liar."

You see, since God created us, he knows best. But keep in mind, I'm not talking about a religion about God. I'm talking about a relationship *with* God. God created you, but we inherited the sin Adam and Eve committed, just like we inherited our DNA. Our blood type doesn't change. I have Syrian blood, which explains my dark skin, but even if I got a blood transfusion, I would still be Syrian!

The reason God created you was to love you. To be with you. To lead you. To live with you. God created us for the same reason we have children. To love them and to be loved by them. He created us so we could express His values and build His kingdom.

But because Adam and Eve believed the lie, we became separated from God. Instead of living with God in His heavenly kingdom and having eternal life with God, we were separated from Him.

And only one thing can bring us back to Him. No amount of

religion, no amount of church, no amount of prayer, no number of chants, no number of candles lit, no amount of good works, or being a "good" person can reconnect you with God.

But God had a plan all along. He knew that Adam and Eve would sin. He already knows what you are going to do in your future. So, He created a plan long ago. He sent His Son Jesus Christ to reconnect us to Him.

Scripture says, "For God so loved the world (that's you and me and all of mankind), that He gave His only begotten Son, that whoever believes in Him should not perish, but have everlasting life."

So, we have a choice. To live the lies of the world or to accept God's Truth and trust Him. When we accept Jesus Christ, God's Son, as our replacement for sin into our heart, Scripture says, "We are saved." Saved from what? Saved from the demonic forces that run our world, saved from the lies of the world. Saved from eternal hell.

I made my choice when I was 27 years old. God has been good to me. I have all nine things because of Him. You can read about it at www.HowardPartridge.org.

When you make a decision for Christ, you will be made brand

new again. Read the last chapter of my book *Think and Be Phenomenal,* and you will see seventy-three scriptures that reveal your new identity.

So, what now? Confess that you are a sinner. We all were before we came to know God's Son. Believe that God is real and that He sent His Son, Jesus, to die for your sins. Confess that you are now God's child and that you trust in Jesus as your Savior. When you do that, He will give you His Holy Spirit, which will help you live by the faith rather than the flesh.

You will then have all nine things that everyone wants out of life. Understand *who* you are and *whose* you are. You are a child of God! You are made in His image. Phenomenal You + Him = Phenomenal Success!

TRUTH #1

God Loves You. You are loved by Him because He made you. He will make you brand new. No matter what bad things you have done, when you know Him, you are good because He is inside of you!

Confess and affirm the following every day…

I Am born to win.

I Am designed for accomplishment.

I Am engineered for success.

After all, God don't make no junk!

I Am a phenomenal product.

Created to be phenomenal, to do phenomenal things, and to have a phenomenal life!

CHAPTER 2
You Aren't Smart Enough to Be Successful

At one point in grade school, we were learning about the Old West. We were to create an art project that would show how people lived back then. Not only was I not smart, I wasn't artistic either. I got a piece of plywood and drew a road and some trees with crayons and then just glued some plastic cowboys and Indians to it. I didn't invest any time at all. I just threw it together.

When the day came to present our projects, I looked around at the other kids' projects, and I was amazed at how good they were. One boy had gotten some hamster cage stuffing and made it look like tall grass. He made some fences from little twigs, and there was a little covered wagon nestled in the corner. The detail was incredible. Surely an adult helped him with his project.

My amazement at their projects quickly turned to embarrassment as I looked at my pitiful creation. I can still feel the pain when I saw the big fat "F" written on the plywood by my teacher. The teacher was disgusted that I would turn in such a terrible project.

I just wasn't very smart. Things didn't get better for me. I was a complete disaster in high school. I skipped school, acted up in class, and even got suspended a couple of times. I hated class. I'm convinced that the only reason I graduated high school was because I was so much trouble, the teachers couldn't stand the thought of putting up with me another year.

I never went to college.

Fast forward to today. I have spoken at Cambridge University in the UK, one of the world's top universities. I was invited to do a TEDx talk at Texas A&M University. I have eight published books before this one. I've had hundreds of articles published, been a keynote speaker at conferences around the world, and have been a guest on hundreds of webinars, podcasts, and radio shows.

I've hosted sixty-four major conferences of my own and held hundreds of workshops around the world and presented thousands of webinars, not to mention the countless times I've been invited to speak at events around the world. I've read at least a thousand books, and I've read through the entire Bible many times.

I've never felt smart, and I still don't feel smart when I compare myself to others. You may be like me. You may not be good in school. You may not feel smart. Or you may be a genius. But having a high IQ doesn't mean we will be met with success. The truth is that we have more information available to us today than ever before. Anything you want to learn, you can learn.

But what's more important than a high IQ is EQ (Emotional Intelligence), which is understanding yourself and understanding how to communicate with others. All of life is about relationships. Your relationship with God, how you see yourself, and how you see others. Zig Ziglar said, "We treat other people the way we see them."

The most important skill you can have is building winning relationships. With God, with others, and with yourself. Reading a book like this and going through a program like Phenomenal You+H helps you to think about yourself, God, and others in the right way.

What that means is that you are aware of what you are doing, why you are doing it, what you are thinking and feeling, and why you are thinking and feeling it.

What is more important than EQ is UQ. That is your Unique Personality, as my friend Dr. Caroline Leaf puts it. Understanding your personality type, your gifts, who God made you to be, and pursuing the purpose that God created you for, rather than the image our negative culture wants to put on you, is key to true success.

Let's remind ourselves of what success is…

Success is becoming who God created you to be. You only have to know the truth to be successful. The truth will set you free. In today's world, you can learn anything you want to learn. Any skill you want to learn is available. Any degree you want is doable.

If I could do it all again, I would have been a better student. I wish I had gone to college. Our son, Christian, went to Texas Tech University in Lubbock, Texas. When we went up to check out the school, I was so impressed with the huge campus. It has an amazing gym and many great buildings. I love to learn now, and I was so inspired with the environment of learning that I turned to my son and said, "I think I want to enroll with you and go to college."

"Dad, you already have everything that people go to college for," he shot back.

Plus, I'm pretty sure he didn't want dear ol' dad sitting in his class with him!

It takes work and study to get to your goal. If you have a goal to be happy, healthy, and prosperous, to have friends, peace of mind, good family relationships, to be secure, to have hope for the future, to love and be loved, it takes work. But I don't want you to just think about the work. I want you to think about your future and what your life can look like if you learn the things you need to learn.

Imagine your life with all nine of the things everyone wants out of life! What would it be worth to make sure you end up with all those things instead of like most people end up? No one really wants to be unhappy, unhealthy, to have money problems, not to have real friends, to have stress, bad family relationships, a meaningless life, and no hope for the future. No one wants to feel unloved, unaccepted, or unimportant.

Zig Ziglar said, "You are what you are and where you are because of what has gone into your mind. You can change what you are and where you are by changing what goes into your mind."

What are you putting into your mind every day? Are you putting in the pure, the positive, and the powerful? Or are you allowing the negative chatter of world events and the social media gossip into your mind? You see, you can control what you look at and, therefore, what goes into your mind.

Of course, in this world, there is a lot going on that we can't avoid seeing, but when you become a positive thinker and constantly remind yourself that you have the mind of Christ (if you know Him), and you were made in God's image, when you remind yourself that you were born to win, you're designed for accomplishment and endowed with the seeds of greatness, that God don't make no junk, that you are a phenomenal product, created to be phenomenal, to do phenomenal things in this life, and to have a phenomenal life – and you accept, adopt, and believe that you plus Him equals phenomenal success, you'll begin to reject the "stinkin' thinkin'," which leads to a very deadly disease called "hardening of the attitudes."

Stinkin' thinkin' might look something like this...

"I can't do it."
"I'm not worthy."
"I have to be perfect."
"I can't make a mistake."
"I'm not good enough."
"Nobody loves me."
When you start thinking like that, you need to think about where you're getting your information. What voices are you

listening to?

Several years ago, I participated in a program through my church called Kids Hope. The program matched church members with "at-risk" kids at a local elementary school. Every week, I went to the school to mentor a student.

My student was 10 years old at the time. Both of his parents were in prison. He was being raised by his grandmother, who had had a terrible childhood. He was unruly at school, and his grandmother was frustrated with his behavior at home.

As I got to know him, I saw his potential. He had a wonderful personality, and he was actually a great kid. His problem was his self-image and the destructive habits that were ingrained in him from an early age.

One day, I arrived at his home room class to begin the mentoring session, and his home room teacher came up to me while the student was across the room getting his backpack. He told me I was wasting my time. He told me that the kid would never change.

I can't tell you how angry I was at that teacher! If we hadn't been in the middle of a classroom full of kids, I would have given him a piece of my mind. And this was his home room teacher where the kid spent most of his day! How dare that teacher decide who has potential and who doesn't! Oh, I was seriously upset!

Remember, we treat people how we see them. How do you think that teacher treated my mentee? Not good. Our modern culture wants to make you think that courage is going with the flow of what everyone else believes. They want to dictate what you should believe. It only takes a quick look around to see that the culture isn't bringing phenomenal success!

You don't even have to be smart to see it. Our government, education system, and media want to mold you to their way of thinking. If you don't believe what they believe, you just aren't smart in their view. And if you believe in Jesus (not just religion), then you're a real bigot!

Isn't that the message you're hearing? Why is it that every other religion, even so-called Christian religion, is accepted, but trusting God through Jesus Christ is mocked? Hmmmm... maybe because it's true? And people are afraid of it because then they don't get to do the things they want to do. Maybe they've been hurt by religion, but they were hurt by religious man, not our holy God.

The world is led by the deeds of the flesh rather than the Spirit of God. God's Word says the deeds of the flesh (the things the world lives by) are sexual immorality, impurity, indecent behavior, idolatry, witchcraft, hostilities, strife, jealousy, outbursts of anger, selfish ambition, dissensions, factions, envy, drunkenness, and carousing. He warns us that those who practice such things will not inherit the kingdom of God. He goes on to say that the fruit of the Spirit is love, joy, peace, patience, kindness, goodness, faithfulness, gentleness, and self-control.

It's your choice. You can listen to the voice of the world or the voice of God. It's just a matter of what outcome you want. Do you want the nine things? Do you want to be a first list person or a second list person? Do you want peace or strife? Do you want to do "your own thing" and suffer the consequences, or do you want to have love, joy, and peace in your life?

It's totally up to you. Mr. Phenomenal is writing to you because I tried the world's way, and it doesn't work. I ended up with a lot of trouble and pain in my life. When I turned my life over to God, He put me on a path where I now enjoy the fruit of the Spirit.

Remember, you are phenomenal. You can live the life you were meant to live. All you need is to know Christ and allow Him to live through you. If you don't know how to start a relationship with God, just confess that you are a sinner, born into original sin, and believe and confess that Jesus Christ, born of a virgin, the only begotten Son of God, died on the cross for your sins.

When you sincerely believe that God's promise is that He will place His Holy Spirit inside of you, you will then be able to live according to the Spirit rather than the flesh. As a result, you'll have the nine things everyone wants out of life, and you'll enjoy the fruit of the Spirit of God.

Once you officially enter God's family, you will be restored to the original intent God had for you. You will have the mind of Christ.

You don't need to search for a new identity on this earth. God knew what He was doing when He created you. Will you still have doubts in the flesh? Yes. Will you still stumble in the flesh? Yes. Will you still feel temptations and desires of the flesh? Yes. But you will be able to overcome because once you have the Spirit, you will be saved for all eternity, and you will have the tools to overcome and live the life God intended you to live. You will be part of God's family too. So, you will have the support, encouragement, and accountability you need through God's family that is all over the world.

And of course, Mr. Phenomenal will be here for you! If you have made a decision for Christ, please let me know.

God gave you an incredible mind. Stop and think about how amazing the human mind is. Think about the technology that man has discovered and the things humans have created. Again, the difference between humans and animals is that humans have a mind. A creative mind.

Jesus was God's first and only Son, and everything was created by Him and through Him. God created the universe, the Earth, and humans through Jesus. He is the Author of Life. And when you know Him, you have the mind of Christ, which means you can now create life.

What does that look like? You can create an atmosphere that builds others up instead of tearing them down. You can create an atmosphere of positive thinking instead of negative thinking. You can choose what you dwell on in your mind and what you don't.

Thinking like God thinks will create a phenomenal future for you. Thinking the way the world thinks will put you in the basket of destruction along with them.

There are many smart people in the world that have done amazing things, but what happens to them when they die? Are they truly happy deep down? Do they have the joy of the Lord? Or are they secretly ashamed about their morality?

Those who fight against morality have something to hide. What is it? They have to admit they are wrong. They have to own up to their own sin. It doesn't mean they are ugly, nasty people. It just means that they don't know Christ.

There are only two kinds of people in the world. Those who know Christ and those who don't. They can argue with that, and they can throw as much water they want onto the Truth, but it will still be Truth.

The way to overcome stinkin' thinkin' is to get a check-up-from-the-neck-up!

TRUTH #2

You were given a phenomenal mind! You are smart! You can learn anything you want to learn. When you know Christ, you have the mind of Christ. You can think like God thinks!

Confess and affirm the following every day...

I Am born to win.

I Am designed for accomplishment.

I Am engineered for success.

After all, God don't make no junk!

I Am a phenomenal product.

Created to be phenomenal, to do phenomenal things, and to have a phenomenal life!

CHAPTER 3

You Aren't Attractive Enough to Be Successful

Recently an 18-year-old "social media influencer" who had 1.4 million followers committed suicide. Why? We put so much emphasis on outward appearances that it creates an unbelievable amount of stress and anxiety for some people.

Throughout history, beauty and brawn have always been desirable for humans, but I think we can all agree that our post-modern culture has brought the need for an amazing outward appearance to an exotic level. So called "influencers" are influencers because of the way they look. Why are we so consumed by the number of followers we have?

And what happens when a social media influencer does something the culture doesn't like? They get crucified. Is that what God has in mind for us? Is that the right way to live? Does that really jive with true purpose in life? I don't think so. I think we are out of balance, and we need to change.

The other end of the spectrum is a whole group of people who have given up on appearances and decided to be sloppy and unclean. They just decided to be lazy. Don't brush my hair, don't brush my teeth, and wear dirty, sloppy clothes.

Finally, there is the outrageous. Everyone has their own taste, but my guess is that you have a definition of what is outrageous and what is not. The more demand there is for attention, the more outrageous one must become to get attention. Shock and awe are the order of the day for entertainers. Get as much attention as you can, and be as controversial as you can.

Why? So, you can get paid more for your posts? So, you can sell more product? So, you can be famous? So, you can feel better about yourself? Meanwhile the *child suicide* rate has doubled in the last decade. Child suicide, a statistic that shouldn't even exist, has doubled. Why? Is there a cultural connection?

How many teenagers have committed suicide because they feel like they are ugly or that they can't measure up to the coolness they see in movie stars and athletes? How much self-doubt and self-loathing has been stirred up by this way of living? And what about the outcome of pride? Thinking you are better than someone else is just another form of a negative self-image.

So, what is the truth? Where is the balance? First, understand that we are all born into a fallen world. Our minds are already infected with selfishness, pride, and many other negative thoughts. We fall victim to the voices in our own heads. Next, culture fuels the fire, causing people to believe they are something they are not.

Think about this for a moment. When God created man, He created them perfect, male and female. Can you imagine how beautiful Adam and Eve were? Then they ate of the tree of knowledge of good and evil. Before that, they only knew the goodness of God. But because God gave them their own free will and they fell into Satan's trap. We all are born with an infected mind.

The knowledge of evil steals the joy from us. Have you ever noticed that a child has a spark in their eyes, but as they fall deeper and deeper into sin, their eyes go dull? Maybe that happened to you. Maybe you never had the spark. Maybe you've had a difficult childhood.

But what does a CHILD of GOD look like? God's creation follows a prescription. But we are born into a fallen world with an infected mind; we begin to believe the lies. We begin to believe that we are supposed to be someone else. Everyone has temptations. Everyone has negative thoughts. Everyone has an infected mind.

But we must choose the truth. As Jesus said in Scripture, the Truth will set you free. He also said, "I Am the Way, the Truth and the Life. No one comes to the Father but through Me." We must fight the negative thoughts we have about ourselves, others, and the culture with God's Word and by allowing the Holy Spirit inside us to guide us. Not our flesh. Not our heart. Scripture says, "The heart of man is desperately wicked – who can know it?" But when you know Christ, you have the mind of Christ. You become a new creature. You have the Holy Spirit inside of you.

Romans Chapter 1 warns us about resisting His ways. He says that He actually gives people over to a depraved mind if they continually resist Him and insist on going their own way. The longer you resist Him, the more infection you have in your mind, and the more likely you'll be carried away by it.

I know those are strong words, but look around. Is our culture really working? Are the world's ideas working? Or are they really just making a handful of people rich and a small percentage of our population more comfortable with their perversions? What kind of world will your children live in if we don't change our ways?

God created man male and female. He wants us to multiply. He wants us to have strong family structures. He knows we need true community to thrive. A community where He is in the middle. The problem is that the religious right and the loose left have radicalized the world and created a huge divide in this world.

Where is truth? In the middle, of course. A relationship with God and understanding that His laws were created for life, not death.

Accept the person God allowed to come into this world. Be the best version of yourself you can be, but understand that you – phenomenal you – is the you that is on the inside, not the outside. Of course, we should groom ourselves and be attractive. Of course, we should be healthy. But changing your looks or choosing to "identify" as something God didn't make you to be is a recipe for disaster.

TRUTH #3

You are beautiful and strong. God doesn't look at outward appearances and neither should we. You are a child of God, made in His image.

Remember who you were created to be...

Let's say it together.

I Am born to win.

I Am designed for accomplishment.

I Am engineered for success.

After all, God don't make no junk!

I Am a phenomenal product.

Created to be phenomenal, to do phenomenal things, and to have a phenomenal life!

CHAPTER 4

You Aren't Connected Enough to Be Successful

The old saying "You pick your friends, but you don't pick your family" is for sure and certain. There seems to be a mindset in our culture that if you're born into the right family, you are automatically set for life. And that if you're born into poverty, you're doomed. All too often, we want to "keep up with the Joneses." The modern-day version is "keeping up with the Kardashians."

As my friend Tom Ziglar likes to point out —it's curious that one child of an abusive alcoholic parent assumes that they too will become an abusive alcoholic because of their upbringing, but another child of the same parent decides that they will never drink because of the abusive alcoholic parent. In other words, since I was raised under the drunken abuse, that should and would be the farthest thing from who I become.

While it's true that one who grows up in a wealthy, connected family has more opportunities for wealth and power, there are two other factors worth noting. First, people who grow up with everything they could ever desire in the way of riches, power, and fame realize they are missing many of the nine things we are talking about in this book.

Money truly doesn't buy happiness. There are plenty of rich girls who have eating disorders or boys who have an inflated ego because their family has money. There are plenty of examples of rich families whose kids are drug addicts. Family problems materialize due to false expectations from both parent and child. Does a person like this truly feel secure and have great hope for the future? Do they truly feel love? I think not.

Second, by the same token, just because a person grows up poor doesn't mean they will be humble and loving. Just because someone grows up in the middle class doesn't guarantee balanced success. Just because someone grows up rich and connected to the right people doesn't mean that person will stay that way.

Think about the "prodigal son" from Scripture. The son who had it all and decided to ask for his inheritance early and squandered it on loose living. Just because someone has an inheritance doesn't mean they will use it for good.

You see, the real difference is in the choosing. You may not choose your family, but you can choose your future. In my own family, my oldest brother was straight as an arrow and began his career at McDonald's at age seventeen, while the next brother in line went to prison at age seventeen. You already know my story. But my younger brother went to college and followed the more traditional path.

The point is that you can choose to be successful or not. Right now, you can make the choice. Speaking of Tom Ziglar, he wrote a book called *Choose To Win – Transform Your Life One Simple Choice at a Time*.

I love this story that he tells … When he was younger, his life goal was to become a professional golfer, and his father, Zig Ziglar, hired one of the top golf instructors in the country to train Tom. Summer was coming up and was packed with lessons.

Mr. Ziglar came home one afternoon and announced that over the summer, he and his wife Jean would be going on a three-week speaking tour in Australia, spanning the entire continent. Tom quickly deduced that it made perfect sense that his parents would need a strong and responsible young man such as him to carry their bags for them.

After his dad was finished sharing the exciting news, Tom finally popped the question…

"Great, Dad! Can I go too?"

Well, in perfect Zig fashion, he didn't answer with a yes or no. Instead, he answered the question with a question.

"Now, son, aren't you training heavily for your upcoming golf tournaments this summer?"

"Yes, sir."

"Is becoming a professional golfer what you really want to do? Do you want to be on the tour next year?" Zig pressed.

"Yes, sir."

"Well, let me ask you a question … will going to Australia for three weeks take you closer to or take you farther from your goal?"

You can probably guess by now that Tom did not go to Australia but stayed home to focus on his bigger, longer term goal. He obviously didn't end up being a professional golfer but has been to Australia twice. In fact, I was with him both times.

I am connected to many people of influence today. But it did not start that way. As you know, I grew up on welfare. Zig

Ziglar himself was born into the second poorest family in Yazoo City, MS. His big dream was to own a butcher shop. Nothing wrong with that, except that he was not thinking big enough for his calling, which was to be a world-renowned inspirational teacher.

Jesus Himself was born to a family without means. Joseph and Mary were simple people. It's not about who you are connected to now. It's about who you *choose* to connect with in the future.

So, how do you connect with people of importance and influence? You help them. Mr. Ziglar's most famous quote and his favorite until the day he passed away is "You can have everything in life you want, if you will just help enough other people get what they want."

Think about that for a second. We've talked about the nine things everyone wants out of life. You can have all those things simply by helping others get those same things. Can you make others happy? No, but you can certainly be unpleasant enough to make others *unhappy!*

Can you help others be healthier? Yes! Statistics have proven that if someone a person is close to has unhealthy habits, chances are that you will adopt those unhealthy habits also. You don't intend to; it just happens. I got on drugs because I wanted to be accepted. Peer pressure is a powerful thing, but you can not only avoid being negatively influenced. You can help others have the nine things!

Can you help others be more prosperous? Of course, you can! Whether that is literally helping someone make money or sharing information and connections yourself, you can definitely help people be more prosperous. That's one of the primary things I do today. But remember, I grew up poor.

Can you help someone have more friends? Yes! The best way to attract friends is to be a friend. Zig taught us that you don't go out looking for friends. You go out to *be* a friend. When you are a true friend to others, you will have a lot of friends and you can introduce them to one another.

By the way, in the business world that's called your "network." Your circle of friends grows, and someone in your group is connected to people who can help you get what you want! You don't go out finding important people and try to convince them to help you. You go out and help everyone you meet. Then when you need something, you have people around you that can help you!

Can you help others have peace of mind? Absolutely! Peace comes from knowing the truth and living by it! That's what this entire book is all about. When you know who you are and *Whose* you are, why you're here on earth, you can have a peace that surpasses understanding. Those around you want that. You can help them overcome their fear and anxiety when you live by faith and share your faith with others.

Can you help others have better family relationships? No doubt about it. Once you're equipped with positive relationship building skills, you can share those with others, and that will help them out.

Can you help people feel more secure? Again, the answer is yes. You can help people understand their value by sharing this information with them. If this book helps you, share it with your friends. Instead of laughing together over how someone else looks in their social media post, help them. Love them. You see, they are struggling with the same self-image issues most people struggle with. Share the pure, positive, powerful truth about who they are and *Whose* they are.

Can you help people have more hope for the future? Of course! Your testimony of hope has an impact on those around you. When you encourage others, you give them fuel. When you live a life of hope, it's contagious!

Can you help more people experience love? To love and to be

loved? Yes! How? Love them!

The point is that you can have everything in life you want, if you will just help enough other people get what they want. Notice the quote says if you *will* help other people. Are you willing to step out and help people? And it says you can have everything in life if you will help *enough* other people get what they want.

Let's break it down:

You (Yes you!)

Can (This is not a maybe.)

Have (What do you want?)

Everything (All nine things)

In Life (remember L.I.F.E. stands for Living In Freedom Every day)

If (Here's the key.)

You (Yes YOU! Not the government or someone else. YOU.)

Will (Are you willing?)

Help (Give, serve, encourage.)

Enough (The number of people you help determines what comes back to you.)

Other (Invest your time into others instead of just yourself.)

People (There are many causes one can give themselves to, but people – God's special creation – is where we should focus our time, money, and energy.)

Get What They Want (They want the same nine things everyone wants: to be happy, healthy, reasonably prosperous, to have friends, to have peace of mind, to have good family relationships, to be secure, to have hope for the future, and to love and be loved.)

Jesus said, "Give, and it will be given back to you, pressed down, shaken together and running over." Imagine buying a bushel of grain, and the merchant shakes the basket around to make sure as much product fits into the basket as possible. Then, he continues to pour it in until it's literally overflowing.

That's what your life can be like. That is what Zig Ziglar's life was like. That is what my life is like. Of course, bad things happen. Of course, the economy can change, and our world is changing every day. Of course, people do bad things to you, but this attitude toward life will prevail in any circumstance of life.

The biggest life lesson I've ever learned is this...

Get around people who have been where you want to be and that have a process to show you the way.

For example, ...
If you want to be godly, hang around people who are godly and who can also share God's Word with you. I have been blessed to have such mentors in my life.

If you want to be more successful financially, get around people who are financially successful and can show you how to do the same. I learned how to build a business from other successful business mentors who had a process for me to follow. When I got my business in debt, I hired a consultant who had a plan to get me out. Now I'm debt free, and my businesses are super profitable.

If you want to be healthier, hang around healthy people who have a proven health program. I got healthy and strong by hiring a certified nutritionist and a personal trainer. I lost all those gains by not meeting with my nutritionist and firing my trainer. I got healthy again with a different plan, and it continues to be an up and down battle for me. But the point is when I have a health coach, I do better.

If you want a specific career, hang around people who have been successful in that career, and of course, go to training to learn how to do it.

Anything you want to learn, find the person who has already been successful and who has a program for you to follow.

A friend of mine recently wrote a wonderful book about having an excellent life. He shared the story of Ben Carson who was raised in poverty yet became a world-renowned surgeon. The reason Ben Carson was successful was because of his mother's tenacity and commitment.

It's true that families who are connected to the power sources get more opportunities than those of us who were born into poverty. However, it is also true that those who are born into privilege aren't always the ones to become successful.

TRUTH #4

You are connected! You are more connected and have more available to you than anyone in history!

Remember, there are so many voices. Listen to your voice as you confess out loud:

I Am born to win.

I Am designed for accomplishment.

I Am engineered for success.

After all, God don't make no junk!

I Am a phenomenal product.

Created to be phenomenal, to do phenomenal things, and to have a phenomenal life!

CHAPTER 5

You Aren't Important Enough to Be Successful

In today's society, success is often defined by the importance of a person's job. Many young people have invested so much of their lives hoping to be a celebrity, a famous musician, or a professional athlete.

We have somehow equated celebrity with success. You may feel insignificant if you don't have a glamorous job or career. The truth is that every one of us is called to a different station in life. We don't decide. God decides. And when we are doing God's will, we will have the nine things everyone wants out of life. And we can help others have the nine things in whatever station we find ourselves. We can encourage others and have influence in their lives.

I had my first real job at 14. I was a dishwasher at a nursing home. I would certainly agree that my gifts would not have been effectively used had I remained a dishwasher for my entire life. However, I had the opportunity to encourage others even in that so-called "menial" job. One of the residents was

Mr. Coleman who had Parkinson's disease. Almost five decades later, I can still feel his hands trembling when I shook his hand. I helped Mr. Coleman with whatever little things he needed, and he loved having someone around to talk to. It made his life happier.

Another resident was a ninety-year-old woman who was deaf and dumb. She was in love with me. Every day, she would seek me out. I will always remember the light-colored wooden door from the dining room to the kitchen that had a small diamond-shaped window. The door was locked after serving time, but this frail little woman, who was too short to see through the window, would rap furiously on the door and jump up and down trying to peek through the little window to see if I was in there.

When I saw her little head bobbing up and down through that little window, I would go and open the door. Her eyes would melt, and she was so happy she found me. Since she couldn't speak or hear, she would just hug me. I reminded her of someone she loved. But the point is that she got tremendous joy from our interactions.

My boss, the woman who hired me, was a great mentor too. She taught me many things about the kitchen, service, and life. I sometimes wonder what would have happened to me had I stayed in touch with her. Surely, she would have been concerned about my rebellious behavior in my teenage years. Maybe I would have become successful sooner.

Washing dishes or working at a fast-food joint may seem like a "menial" job to some, but there is no such thing as a menial job. And someone who works a job like that is not a loser. The key is to help others.

The voices we hear from the media make you feel like a loser if you don't have it all. Listen closely. Is the media pure? Is the entertainment industry pure? Do they truly have your best interest in mind? I don't think so. So, what's the point? The point is that we all have to start somewhere. And the bigger point is that you can have it "all." You may be able to get money and maybe even fame following the ways of the world, but you won't be happy. Why do mega-rich, famous stars commit suicide?

The bigger point is that if we open our eyes to the truth, we can learn a great deal about life, ourselves, and others through even entry level jobs. If you can start out with a better, higher paying job, then by all means do it. You may not always love your job, but you can earn the right to choose your job as you bring more value to the marketplace.

My oldest brother started working at McDonald's at age seventeen. It was his first job. And as it turns out, *his* only job for his entire life. He became a store manager, then a regional manager, and eventually got the opportunity to buy his own McDonald's store. He sold that store and became a multi-millionaire. He and his wife raised a phenomenal family, are great people of faith, and serve on mission trips. They have the nine things because they helped enough others get the nine things. Was it easy? No. Was it always fun? No. But the outcome was amazing.

Don't let any voices tell you that your job doesn't matter. Regardless of your post in life, you are in a position to help others and to help yourself. Your work makes our world a better place, regardless of what it is. You do not have to be a social media influencer to have a phenomenal life.

So, how do you move up the ladder? How do you find the right work for you? How far can you go? How far should you go?

The first thing to think about is balance. Does the work you're thinking about honor God? Does it honor your family? Will it help you become a better person? Will it help you with the nine things? The voices may tempt you to be a social media influencer or celebrity, but your goal is not fame or fortune. It's the nine things. Stay balanced.

The second thing to think about is the value of work. Hard work is rewarding. While there is nothing wrong with inventing a piece of software and becoming mega-rich (think Google), or creating disruptive technology and becoming a billionaire (think Elon Musk or Steve Jobs), there is equally nothing wrong with simply working hard in a more traditional role. Do you want to be a business owner? Work hard at whatever you do. There is no such thing as an overnight success. There is no such thing as money for nothing. Hard work builds values. Value hard work.

Third, meaningful work is inspiring. Whatever work you do, whatever business you build, try to understand the meaning behind it. A brick layer is not laying brick. He is building a home or business that will house people and give them a wonderful place to work. Someone doing data entry is not just entering information into a computer, she is helping someone make a difference in the world. Learn to look at the purpose of work. What does it do for others? Remember Mr. Coleman and the deaf and dumb ninety-year-old woman at my dishwasher job. Fourth, whether you are on the top floor or the bottom floor, you have an opportunity to touch someone next to you. Many years ago, I was working as a waiter at night to support my cleaning business in the daytime. One night, we learned that the popular band ZZ TOP was coming in for a private party after their concert.

Everyone was excited except for Clint, our one-man band. You know the guy who has a guitar in his hand, a bass drum that he taps with a pedal, and a harmonica on a stand near his lips? That guy. He was so worried about playing in front of these amazing and world-famous rock stars. "They don't want to hear me play!" Clint moaned. He was going to pack up his gear and go home. "Don't worry about it," I said. "It will be fine. Just do your thing." I continued to encourage him.

A little while later, a half-dozen Texas Rangers on motorcycles with blue lights in full strobe escorted three long black limos into the parking lot. In strolled the long-bearded Billy Gibbons, Dusty Hill, and Frank Beard (oddly, the only one without a beard).

Clint was tense as he began to strum the guitar to the beat of that base drum. That night, Clint Black was discovered by ZZ TOP's manager. If you don't know the name Clint Black, he is a very successful country star today.

This story may tempt you to be the next Clint Black, but keep two things in mind. One, Clint spent many years playing his heart out in clubs and little restaurants like that one just to keep food on the table. Like me, he probably worked another job in the daytime to keep his passion in play.

Second, I was in a position to encourage him. Not because I had an important position. I was a waiter. In a restaurant that wasn't significant in the community. Whatever position you play on the team – whatever role you fulfill, you have an opportunity to influence others positively.

By understanding your God-given potential, your gifts, your goals and purpose, and what a balanced life looks like, you will make better career choices. In fact, I became a professional waiter and ended up working at one of the top restaurants in town. I wore a real tuxedo to work (not one of the tuxedo-look-alike outfits some servers wear). I learned the art of table side cooking and serving Houston's most prominent citizens, celebrities, and world leaders. It was the highest-level service experience ever, taken to an art form.

But that was not to be my career. As you know, I started my first business out of the trunk of my car. A fellow waiter was my first customer, and the restaurant itself became a client. And as you may also know, that business is the most successful of its kind in the Houston area and is a model people follow worldwide.

And as you definitely know, the success of that business launched my career and calling to be an international business coach helping business owners, leaders, and their teams and families all over the world. From a dishwasher to international business coach and author, I was able to use my influence to help others have the nine things. As a result, I have the nine things myself.

Of course, the next obvious question is how much you should make at your job or in your business. I'll cover this in the next chapter. Your job, your career, or your business will likely be your main (and maybe only) source of income, so it deserves its own chapter.

Remember, the key is balance. Mr. Ziglar always taught us that "success is living a balanced life." Of course, to get where you want to go you'll need to sacrifice. Just don't sacrifice your values. Don't sacrifice your family or faith. You cannot expect to have phenomenal success by short cutting the process. You cannot expect to be successful by accident. You cannot expect other people to hand you the keys. You cannot expect to be truly successful if you don't love others and treat them with the respect they deserve.

And to quote Mr. Ziglar one more time, "You were born to win, but in order to be the winner you were born to be, you must plan to win and prepare to win before you can expect to win. But when you plan to win and prepare to win, you can expect to win."

Remember, there are so many voices. Especially in the area of career.

TRUTH #5

You are important! There is only ONE you!

Confess out loud, once again:

I Am born to win.

I Am designed for accomplishment.

I Am engineered for success.

After all, God don't make no junk!

I Am a phenomenal product.

Created to be phenomenal, to do phenomenal things, and to have a phenomenal life!

CHAPTER 6
You Aren't Rich Enough to Be Successful

If there is any one single thing people use to categorize people in the success column today, it has to be how rich they are. Let's face facts. Everyone wants to do well financially. We all want to be able to pay our bills and to buy the things we want to.

The problem is you have probably listened to the wrong voices when it comes to money. If you are like most people, you have feelings about money that are emotional and out of balance. Everyone seems to want more money but are probably envious of those who have it. The subject of money can cause lots of stress and anxiety.

Everyone deserves to have a non-judgmental, balanced view of money.

Since I have money and I've been poor, I'll try to help you have a more balanced view on this issue. Better than that, I'll share what Mr. Ziglar had to say about it. Remember, he was also poor but became rich. And most importantly, I'll share what

I've learned from the ultimate source: what Scripture has to say about money.

The first thing I want you to know is that the title of this chapter is a LIE. You do not need to be rich to be successful. Jesus Himself didn't own anything. But money was involved in His mission. Otherwise, there wouldn't have been a money bag to be stolen by Judas who betrayed Him. By the same token, no one should expect someone else to take care of their financial responsibilities. Personal responsibility is the key to a positive, balanced financial life.

Jesus didn't require anyone to give to His ministry. If Jesus owned anything, it would have compromised His mission. But money was involved in carrying out the mission. Judas had to steal the money bag because Scripture prophesied it years before it happened. But money was used to fulfill the mission. Even though Jesus could manufacture money anytime He wanted (like the time He made a coin appear in the mouth of a fish), the mission was mostly funded by His followers. A rich man named Joseph of Arimathea provided the tomb where Jesus was buried, and he provided the expensive perfumes and spices used in the burials of the day.

Did Mother Teresa have a huge portfolio garnered from a phenomenal career? No. Nelson Mandela? Nope. Martin Luther

King? Not. But money was a tool that was used in all these missions. Many of the mega-successful people you know of didn't have money when they started.

You don't even have to have a "big job" to be successful financially. You don't have to be a celebrity to be successful financially. You don't have to be a professional athlete. Most young people would probably say something like, "I want to be able to pay my bills and not have to worry about money." That's possible, but it doesn't happen by accident. It happens through intention.

You might say, "Howard, I want to be super-rich! I want to be so rich that I don't have to worry about *anything*! I want to be able to buy whatever I want anytime I want."

My answer? Great! There are no limits. The only limit is in your mind. You are only limited by your imagination. The key is what do you want and why? If you want to be mega-rich so you can boss other people around and get what you want so you don't have to be nice to others and live the lifestyle of the rich and famous, just because you think it would be cool, and you will be cool, means you have likely missed the entire point of this book: YOUR VALUE.

The amount of money you make has nothing to do with your inherent God-given value. Regardless of whether you are financially rich or poor in this world, you are a PHENOMENAL PRODUCT.

Let's take a moment to have the "phenomenal talk" as my sweet friend Alexandra started calling it. The phenomenal talk goes like this:

Me to a stranger: "Did you know that you're phenomenal?"

The responses range from "Thank you" to "No, I didn't" to "Yes, I do."

Regardless of the response, I say: "Do you know why you are phenomenal? Because God made you, and everything He makes is phenomenal. Especially humans! You were created in God's very image!"

I was telling one of my clients about the "phenomenal talk," and he told me a story about going into a store with a friend who was a youth pastor. At check out, his friend picked up the scanner the cashier was using and said, "If I scanned you, what value would your register show?" Wow, I thought that was powerful.

The fact is that regardless of how much money you have or don't have – regardless of how much money you make, or the number of houses or cars you have– it does not change your value one bit!

Money is a tool. You can use it for good or you can use it for ruin. It does not care. One of the reasons we must be careful not to put too much comfort and security into money is we don't control its value. The value of a dollar is determined by world events. The value of real estate, stocks, and any currency are determined by world events.

By the same token, we should use this tool in a balanced way. I have used money in all the wrong ways. I blew my money. I got into major debt. I got my company into major debt. Fortunately, my wife was very good with money, and I had help from others and got my business super profitable. Since then, I've made better business decisions and better personal financial decisions.

The result is that I am debt-free and have less stress. I'm blessed with not only the material things like great houses and amazing cars, the opportunity to travel and the ability to buy just about anything I want, I've been able to give away a lot of money! I give money to people who are in trouble, to great causes, and to my church.

Making money is one of my talents, and I understand that everyone doesn't have that gift. So my goal is to make as much money as possible to help as many people as I can. Is it okay to buy some cool toys along the way? Of course! As long as it doesn't affect the other things on the list of things everyone wants. As long as others aren't suffering because of your spending. Balance is the key. Be rich toward God, stay out of debt, and be wise. Be faithful to your mission in life.

If you had a child who worked extremely hard and was a blessing to others, would you tell your child they couldn't buy a toy? Of course not. Why would God deny us a few simple pleasures of life as long as they don't become idols?

But because humans can easily slip into the flesh, we have to be mindful and prayerful. Recently, I went on an unusual buying frenzy of luxury cars. These cars are so nice that I found myself being overprotective of them. I don't want them scratched or damaged in any way. My wife warned me not to make them an idol. She is right. At the same time, we should properly care for the things we have.

Most importantly, we should be grateful for any and all success that comes our way. Even if we worked very hard for it, let us not forget that God gave us the gifts, the ideas, and the opportunities. As the Apostle Paul said, "Be content with food and covering." Anything beyond that is an overflow of blessings.

Mr. Ziglar had a few things to say about gratitude also…

"Out of all the attitudes one can acquire, surely the attitude of gratitude is certainly the most important and the most life changing."

He also said, "The more you are grateful for what you have, the more you will have to be grateful for."

Let's get back to the subject of money.

Mr. Ziglar said, "Money isn't the most important thing in life, but it is reasonably close to oxygen on the 'gotta-have-it-scale.'" The fact is that in this world, just to have food and covering, you need money!

He always said he likes the things money could buy – the fact that he could take the Redhead (his wife, Jean) out to dinner, that he owned two houses and drove a nice car – that he could enjoy a country club membership. "But I love the things money can't buy," he continued. "Money can buy you a companion but not a friend. It can buy you a house but not a home. It can buy you a bed, but not a good night's sleep."

And what does Scripture say?

God's Word informs us to "owe no one anything but to love them." Personal, unsecured debt is a bad deal. It is so freeing to get debt free. Getting rid of the stress and anxiety that comes with debt is one major benefit. The other is the savings! That's right! If you ever look at how much in finance charges you're paying over and above when you put something on credit, it's outrageous.

That money could be in your pocket, or it could be used to help someone. It could be used for a good cause.

There are many Scriptures that some well-meaning religious people like to get legalistic about. They twist and turn God's Word to get them off the hook to take care of their own responsibilities. Why is it that people who cry foul when someone is prosperous are themselves deep into debt and won't improve their own financial situation? Even when the opportunity is right in front of them? They continue on with paying ridiculous credit card fees and cry about not having enough money because they ate out too much.

They complain about not making enough money but refuse to take on a second job or any other kind of opportunity. At the same time, they would gladly take your help for free. Is that faith? Or is it fear? Remember that legalistic religion is all about fear, not faith.

Scripture warns us, "The love of money is the root of all sorts of evil." Some have misinterpreted this verse to say, "The love of money is the root of all evil." The correct translation is "all sorts of evil." The love of money is the issue. If you love money more than God or people, you're in trouble.

Jesus said, "You cannot have two masters. You cannot love God and money. One will become master. You will love the one and hate the other. Remember, it's about balance. Financial success can be a huge temptation for sure. On the other side of the coin, people somehow use this as an excuse to be in debt, to ignore opportunities, and to dismiss opportunities to do better financially. They bury their heads in the sand when it comes to this subject of money instead of getting the right perspective about it. The reason for that is there is so much internal emotional turmoil attached to money. Maybe growing up, they experienced a lot of pain surrounding money.

A scene in *The Pursuit of Happyness* starring Will Smith (based on the true story of Chris Gardener who emerged from homelessness to become a successful stockbroker) captured the emotion perfectly. He was standing in line at a men's shelter with his little boy in tow as a luxury convertible turned the corner. The four passengers were laughing and having a wonderful time as they drove by. You could see the pain on his face as the car passed.

A scene like that can make you feel uneasy about having nice things. Today, Chris has a net worth of *seventy-million dollars.* Assuming that actually happened in real life, and assuming that Chris actually felt that way, who's to say that those people in the convertible didn't give a lot of their money away? Or what if although they seemed happy deep down inside, they were wretched? Why do rich and famous movie stars commit suicide? Maybe the owner of that convertible was deep in debt.

We cannot judge others. Scripture says, "To their own master, they stand or fall." Regardless of whether we are rich or poor, we should wake up, get up, dress up, and show up in the best way possible, every single day. That's what Chris Gardner did. He got up and showed up, and he never gave up. He found a way.

Success doesn't make us, and failure doesn't break us. It's a journey.

Most people carry a ton of emotional baggage when it comes to money. But many times, money is just the manifestation of deeper issues. Jealousy, pride, guilt, desire for power, or the need to be recognized. And you can be sure that every human has some element of an imbalance in the flesh.

So, what can you do?

Be aware of what you believe and what you feel. Know what is true and what is not true. Perhaps growing up, you felt hurt that other people seemingly had wonderful lives while you were struggling. Perhaps you felt superior because your family was wealthy.

Back to Scripture for a moment. There is a story about a rich, young ruler who asked Jesus how to be saved. Jesus said, "Keep the commandments." The rich, young ruler replied, "I've kept them since my youth." (I might mention that he just lied because that is impossible for any human except Jesus.)

When Jesus heard this, he said to him, "One thing you still lack. Sell all that you have and distribute to the poor, and you will have treasure in heaven; and come, follow me." But when he heard these things, he became very sad for he was extremely rich. Jesus, seeing that he had become sad, said, "How difficult it is for those who have wealth to enter the kingdom of God! For it is easier for a camel to go through the eye of a needle than for a rich person to enter the kingdom of God." Those who heard it said, "Then who can be saved?" But he said, "What is impossible with man is possible with God."

Some say that the eye of the needle that Jesus spoke of was a small gate in the wall of the city which travelers who arrived after dark would have to pass through since the main city gates were closed. If one was rich, their camels would be carrying lots of goods. They would have to unload the camel and get him on his knees to crawl through the small gate.

Whether that is true or not, I personally know many people who are wealthy who love God. The key is being "rich toward God." Are you rich toward God? Jesus said there are only two commandments. One is to "love the Lord your God with all your heart, soul, mind, and body." And the second one is to "love others as you love yourself." He said all of the Law and the Prophets (all of God's Word) hinge on these two things.

The real question for you is, "How much money should you make? How much money should you have?" The answer is, "How much money do you need to fulfill the vision you have for your life?" You see, in order to know "how much," you need to know *what* you are supposed to do with your life and *why* you are supposed to do it. Then you can determine how much.

The amount of money you need is the amount of money you need. Simple, but profound. The amount of money you need is the amount of money you need to fulfill your vision for your life.

First, realize that money doesn't make the person; it *reveals* the person. As you observe your feelings and actions, do a little self-coaching to discover why you feel the way you do. What is the truth of the matter?

Second, understand that money is a tool. Don't allow the tool to control you. Just because you have a hammer, is everything around you a nail? No. Just like any tool, it's in your toolbox to use when you are building something that requires that tool.

What are you building? What are you trying to do? Why? Does it honor God? Is it in balance with the rest of your priorities?

Your belief about money (and about everything for that matter) will determine your philosophy about it. I developed this money philosophy for myself....

1. Make a lot of money. My philosophy is that there are many things I need to do in my short time on this planet. Money is the currency that gets things done. So, I need to make a lot of money to do the things I want to do.

2. Give a lot of money. When I was broke and in debt, I couldn't help people like I do today. If I don't make money, I can't give money.

3. Invest a lot of money. Even though our eternal security isn't dependent on money, being wise with the money you make

can make you money. For example, I own several houses. Every one of them has increased in value; not to mention, each one has served others in one way or another. But even if I didn't use the things I own to bless others, my personal opinion is that as long as we are rich toward God, He is okay with me using part of it to buy stuff. I could be wrong, and I may not have as big a mansion in heaven as a result, but I might be right. What I do know is that religious bigots who call themselves Christians rail against people who have nice things. As Mr. Ziglar would say, "Were the diamonds made for Satan's crowd?" Believers will inherit and rule the earth. It might be good for us to learn how to be good stewards while we are here.

4. Spend a lot of money. When I built my second dream home, although I felt God helped me all along the way, even doing miracles that helped me acquire the property and build the house (I tell the entire story in my book *Discover Your Phenomenal Dream Life*), I felt like maybe I was investing too much on myself. My dream. A friend reminded me that building that house would provide many jobs, and it has. It has also been a wonderful place of rest for us and many others who visit. Spending money, whether it's a house or a car or clothing, creates jobs and helps the economy. The balance for me is to make sure I am giving to those in need, and good causes as well, which I do consistently.

There are many ways to make money. When I was a kid, I cut grass to make money. I sold stuff door to door. I always had a job. When I was 23, I started my own business. There are many types of small businesses you can start with little to no money. Whatever you do, use this tool called 'money' wisely.

Finally, let me share this truth… If you are reading this book, you are rich enough to be successful. If you have access to learning, you can accomplish anything. I had Brian Tracy, one of the top success teachers of our day, speaking at my conference a few years ago. After he spoke to the large group, I asked him to sit with some of our VIPs. There was a young man in the audience who expressed an interest in real estate and asked Brian how he could be successful in that field.

Brian's response was, "You can learn everything you want to know about real estate and become a multi-millionaire if you want to. The knowledge is available. You just have to go learn it." Incidentally, Brian Tracy is a multi-millionaire himself, but at one time he was homeless.

It doesn't matter where you come from (Lower Alabama for me. The second poorest family in Yazoo City, MS, for Zig Ziglar), it matters where you are going. What do you want to do? What is God calling you to? What is your passion? What problem do you want to solve in the world?

God has a purpose for your life. You do not have to be broke, in debt, and have the kinds of money problems most people have. Be faithful with little, and God will give you more to take care of. Money is a tool. It's a resource. It all belongs to God. You are just the steward. Understand how it works and use it wisely.

Remember, there are so many voices. And there are many loud voices when it comes to the "almighty dollar." Your value has nothing to do with how much money you make. You are rich enough to be successful.

TRUTH #6

You are RICH! You have everything you need to be successful. You just have to go out and get it.

Confess out loud, once again:

I Am born to win.

I Am designed for accomplishment.

I Am engineered for success.

After all, God don't make no junk!

I Am a phenomenal product.

Created to be phenomenal, to do phenomenal things, and to have a phenomenal life!

CHAPTER 7

You Aren't Free Enough
to Be Successful

A friend of mine shared a message at church about his father who was a soldier in World War II. He had been captured by the Nazis and was in a prison camp along with others from the Allied Forces. Every morning, they woke up to barbed wire fences and heavily armed German soldiers who made sure no one escaped.

But one day, they woke up, and the guards were gone. And the gates of the prison camp were wide open! They were free! But then fear kicked in. Was this some kind of sick joke? If they left, would they encounter their captives just outside the camp and be shot? And if their captors were gone, what about the townspeople close by? Would they come after them with pitchforks?

They were free, but they were still held captive in their minds. They sat down and waited. At some point, the United States military rescued them. This story reminds me that we are only captives in our own minds and our own hearts. Even if we are locked up physically.

One of my favorite movies of all time is *Braveheart*. William Wallace, a Scottish commoner, took on the oppressive English government that was wrongly occupying Scotland. He also had to fight the corrupt politicians in Scotland that were considered "noblemen." He led his untrained militants into battle and beat the most powerful army in the world, time and time again.

But he was double-crossed and captured. In a dark dungeon, the incoming queen who loved him begged him to confess his loyalty to the wicked English king to spare his life. His response was one of the most moving, inspiring quotes I've ever heard. "Every man dies. Not every man really lives."

The next day, he was wheeled out for his torture and beheading in front of a jeering crowd. The executioner showed off his set of deadly tools. The crowd replied with louder cries. The grim reaper then asked Wallace if he was now ready to confess his "sin" against the king. He was silent.

After torturing him to the point of near death and to utter exhaustion, the killer was sure he had gotten his victim to the point of giving in. With a hand motion, he quieted the crowd. "The prisoner wishes to speak," he announced. As William Wallace tried to regain his strength to speak, as he cleared his throat, anticipation grew in the crowd. Surely, they were about to witness a resignation. The pain had to be too great. Wallace lifted his head a bit and growled F-R-E-E-E-E-E-D-O-M!

As a young person, you may feel that you don't have any real freedom. Maybe you feel restricted by rules in your house, at school, or in society. I understand. I felt the same way. I wanted to do my own thing. But what I realized is that you don't get true freedom by demanding your own way. You don't get freedom by rebelling. You don't get freedom by forcing others to go along with your ideas because "this is just the way you are."

Most people who read this book are in the U.S. and other "free countries." And we can debate how much freedom we have as a nation, but your nationality, whether free or not, doesn't dictate your freedom.

Your mind does. Your heart does. Was William Wallace free? Was Nelson Mandela free? Was Corrie ten Boom or Anne Frank or Viktor Frankl free? It all depends on what you call freedom. As human beings, we have the freedom of thought, the freedom to create. The freedom to imagine. And in most cases, we have at least some national freedoms left. That's another story, but it doesn't matter where you are, you are free.

There's a Scripture I love in the book of Galatians that says, "It was for freedom you were set free. Only use that freedom to serve others." Remember, this entire book is about how to get everything you want out of life. How to have the nine things everyone wants in life: to be happy, healthy, reasonably prosperous, to have friends, to have peace of mind, to have good family relationships, to be secure, to have hope for the future, to love and to be loved.

It all starts and ends with love. When you love God, you will be happy. When you love others, you will feel loved. Freedom is when you decide to love others even when they have done you wrong. When they have lied to you – or harmed you in some way. That's true love.

There is freedom in love. It doesn't matter whether we are nationally free or not. That's a bonus. You see, there are two places in your being that no one can touch except for you and God alone. Your mind and your heart. When you receive God's love, you will have His peace. Know Him. Know Peace. No Him. No Peace.

When you love Him and love others, you will have freedom. Did Jesus have freedom when he went to the cross? Yes! God was in control. Did Nelson Mandela have freedom when he was jailed? Yes! God was in control.

You see, freedom happens in your mind and in your heart. You have the bonus that you have more freedom than others. The fact is that if you are reading this book, you are free. Whether you are in jail or sitting in one of your family's fabulous homes, you are free enough to be successful. Because freedom happens in your mind and in your heart.

You get to choose what you do with that freedom. You can use it to sit and scroll through your social media all day. You can use it to make fun of other people's looks. You can use it to be outrageous and make everyone bow down to your wishes. You can use your freedom to be a slob and put every unhealthy thing imaginable into your body.

You can use your freedom to not work, to complain that life isn't fair. To loathe other people because the one you want to love you doesn't. You can use your freedom to rebel against your parents because they are dumb and old-fashioned and aren't "up" on things. You can use your freedom to curse others. You can use your freedom to rail against people who have more than you or don't agree with you. You can use your freedom to be a prisoner of your own making. You can use the free will that God gave you to rebel against Him and to run from Him because you exercised your freedom to not read the Scriptures and believe the lies other people have told you. It's your choice. You can choose to lump Christianity in with false Christian religions. You are free to choose what you believe in your heart and what you think in your mind.

Or you can choose to accept the truth. As Jesus said, "The truth will set you free." He also said that He IS the Truth, the Way, and the Life. That no man comes to the Father but through Him. You can use your freedom to actually come to know God rather than believe the lies about Him.

You can use your freedom to think for yourself based on what God says, not what your social media feed says. You can use your freedom to be healthy. You can use your freedom to be a friend rather than demand others to be your friend. You can use your freedom to be at peace. You can use your freedom to love your family, no matter what, and to be patient with them. You can use your freedom to pursue the career that is right for you. You can use your freedom to make the amount of money that is right for you. And you can use your freedom to be free in your mind, in your heart, and to help others experience their own freedom.

The fact that you got this far in this book (assuming you did), tells me that I have your attention. Remember that this book is about what you want…

To be happy

To be healthy

To be prosperous

To have real friends

To have peace of mind

To have good family relationships

To be secure

To have hope for the future

To love and to be loved

As a person who at one time had none of those nine things and today has all those things and, more importantly, as a person who has helped many other people around the world have these things, I am testifying to you that the one and ONLY way to get there is to…

Help enough other people get what they want.

The "golden rule" is still true today. "Do unto others as you would have them to do unto you." Give, and it will be given back to you, pressed down, shaken together, and running over.

TRUTH #7

You are FREE! You are free in your head and your heart. No one can affect your mind and heart without your permission. You can choose.

Let's confess together one last time…

I Am born to win.

I Am designed for accomplishment.

I Am engineered for success.

After all, God don't make no junk!

I Am a phenomenal product.

Created to be phenomenal, to do phenomenal things, and to have a phenomenal life!

ACKNOWLEDGMENTS

God gives visions, and His people carry out the vision. God first gave me the vision for Phenomenal You+H way back in 2012. I thought about it a lot but didn't do anything with it.

Several years later, I felt that I was supposed to hear something from God, but I couldn't quite dial in what it was. I took four days off to walk on my beach and pray. I didn't do any work. No social media. I didn't talk to anyone. I told my team I would be off the grid. My wife and my assistant were the only two to contact me and only if there was an emergency. Of course, I did talk to my wife once a day.

I walked up and down the three mile stretch of beach, seeking God's voice daily. On the third day, I felt led to my office where I had my stack of Ziglar Planners. I felt there was something there that I needed to see.

As I began to thumb through the pages, I came across the idea of Phenomenal You+H from way back in 2012. It jumped out at me like a ring of fire was around it. I knew immediately that was what I was searching for.

On the fourth day, I thought about what a program might look like and how I could help young people. The original idea was an afterschool program where kids would be dropped off after school somewhere like a church facility or community center, and they would learn the phenomenal way of life. Perhaps local businesses would sponsor and mentor as well.

Meanwhile, I was thinking about not holding my annual Destin Beach Retreat because it doesn't make money. It's expensive to stay here, and it's not an easy place to get into and out of. Plus, everyone isn't a beach lover like me.

I mentioned to my client Carlos Campos that I was thinking of not holding it, and he shot back, "You better have it!" I was taken back a bit. "My boys will be highly upset," he continued. You see, his two young boys, Samuel and Daniel, had been to my retreat. They got the phenomenal message.

They returned to school after the summer and began telling their classmates that "they were phenomenal." Both of them became class president that year! So, I sent an email to my membership to let them know not only would I be holding it, but that we were going to have something special for young people. Ninety-seven people attended, and over half of them were kids!

After making that decision, I was at Ziglar headquarters and remembered that Zig had a course for youth called I CAN. It was in hundreds of schools many years ago. Laurie went into the depths of the archives and emerged with a humongous I CAN binder. "This was Zig's dream," she remarked as she slowly handed it over to me. With tears in my eyes, I wiped the dust off the cover and began to go through it. I shared some of the content with the kids, and they loved it!

Then, I invited two families that have followed Zig for many years to help teach the course. Jamie Hallas and Sarah Marion stepped up to the plate. We then began a weekly POD called Phenomenal You+H with their two families. Daniel and Esther May Marion now lead that group.

To learn more about this work and to join a weekly POD to get the support, encouragement, and accountability we all need to move forward in life, please visit www.phenomenalyouth.com And of course, thank you to Alan and Debbie Hunter for allowing me to share Jessica's story.

Let me end my part of this book with a little poem about life from 11-year-old Jessica.

Life

Everybody has a purpose,
not one is the same
But everyone is simular,
in a certain way.
We all come on earth
to do something spectacular.
And we all leave this earth,
to a better place to stay.
We might be leaving loved ones,
that will miss us very much.
But when we get up to heaven,
there will be people waiting for us.
Life is so, so grand,
so don't lose a second of it.
Then just get out there,
and have some fun.

Poem By:
Jessica Hunter